DEATH VALLEY NATIONAL PARK

A TRUE BOOK

by
David Petersen

Children's Press®
A Division of Grolier Publishing
New York London Hong Kong Sydney
Danbury, Connecticut

For Becky Abbey

Reading Consultant
Linda Cornwell
Learning Resource Consultant
Indiana Department of
Education

Death Valley is in east-
central California, and
extends into Neveda.

Library of Congress Cataloging-in-Publication Data

Petersen, David, 1946–
    Death Valley National Park / by David Petersen.
        p.   cm.   —   (A true book)
    Includes index.
    Summary: Depicts the scenery and wildlife at Death Valley National Park
and recounts the efforts to save the area from destruction by mining.
    ISBN 0-516-20049-6 (lib. bdg.)   0-516-26095-2 (pbk.)
    1. Death Valley National Park (Calif. and Nev.)—Juvenile literature.
[1. Death Valley National Park (Calif. and Nev.)] I. Title.
[F868.D2P4 1996]
979.4'87—dc20   96-635
                                                              CIP
                                                              AC

Contents

Death Valley National Park is best-known for its sand dunes; but many other features of the park are just as fascinating.

Death Valley National Park

On the edge of the Mojave Desert, along the border between California and Nevada, lies Death Valley National Park—one of the hottest and driest places on Earth. On July 10, 1913, Furnace Creek sizzled at a

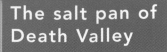

The salt pan of
Death Valley

world-record 134 degrees
Fahrenheit (57 degrees
Celsius)—in the shade. Out on
the barren, salty desert floor,
called the salt pan, there are
no trees, no plants, and no
animals. But there's more to
Death Valley than the salt pan.

The park, which covers almost 2.7 million acres (1.1 million hectares), is larger than most national parks, and half as big as the state of Delaware. This huge valley includes several very different environments.

Death Valley from Dante's View

Badwater, the lowest spot in the western hemisphere (top) and the Panamint Range, which contains Telescope Peak (bottom)

For example, the lowest place in the western hemi-sphere—and the hottest—is the Badwater region of Death Valley. But from Badwater, which lies 282 feet (86 meters) below sea level, you can look up to snow-covered Telescope Peak in the Panamint Range. It rises 11,049 feet (3,368 m) above sea level. This is more than two miles (3.2 kilometers) higher than Badwater!

The distance between Badwater and Telescope Peak is more than two miles (three kilometers).

The temperature difference between these two extremes can be 50 degrees Fahrenheit (10 degrees C) or more. A variety of plants and animals have adapted to life in these different environments.

Life in Death Valley

The wildlife of lower Death Valley includes insects, lizards, snakes, birds, and small mammals such as kangaroo rats, ground squirrels, and jackrabbits. Feeding on these small animals are larger predators, such as coyotes, kit foxes, owls, and roadrunners.

Animals found in Death Valley include (clockwise, from top) the kit fox, ground squirrel, roadrunner, and collared lizard.

Desert bighorn sheep live on the cooler slopes of the mountains.

High on the mountain slopes, the environment becomes cooler and more moist, allowing a greater variety of plant life to thrive. Death Valley's most unusual mammal, the shy desert bighorn sheep, is found here.

Desert trumpet plant (left);
Sidewinder rattlesnakes (above)
move sideways over the ground.

In all, more than 600 species of plants, 230 species of birds, 19 species of snakes (including the sidewinder rattlesnake), 17 species of lizards, and dozens of mammals live in Death Valley. The park is also home to three species of rare desert pupfish.

Devils Hole Pupfish

The pupfish that live in Death Valley National Park are called Devils Hole pupfish. They are 1½ inches to 2½ inches (4 to 6 centimeters) long and can survive in water up to 112 degrees Fahrenheit (44 degrees Celsius). The females are brown and white colored; the males are blue and purple colored. Pupfish can flip from one small pool to another, and some are able to hibernate in mud during the winter.

People in Death Valley

The first people to occupy Death Valley were American Indians called the Nevares Spring people. They lived about 7,000 years ago.

Other native people came later, most recently the Shoshone, who were living near Furnace Creek when the first white people arrived.

Petroglyphs are drawings done by the American Indians who lived in Death Valley thousands of years ago.

For 7,000 years, American Indians survived in Death Valley. These desert people had few needs—food, clothing, water, and shelter. In the

American Indians used rocks like this to grind up their food.

mid-1800s, travelers began passing through Death Valley. They were European people who were new to the desert. Unlike the American Indians, the newcomers had no idea how to survive in this harsh environment.

According to legend, one of these early pioneers, a prospector on his way to the California gold fields in 1849, coined the name "Death Valley."

Other pioneers agreed with this name. Within Death Valley are places called Badwater, the Devil's Cornfield, Last Chance Range, the Devil's Golf Course, and the Funeral Mountains. Even though Death Valley was

Devil's Cornfield

a difficult place to live, some prospectors returned to Death Valley in search of gold and silver. Instead, they found borax.

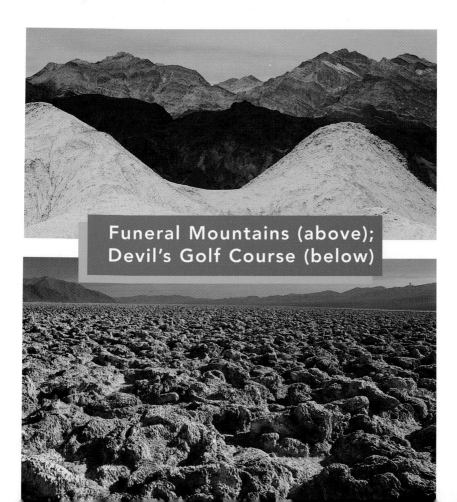

Funeral Mountains (above);
Devil's Golf Course (below)

The Borax Boom

Borax is a white, powdery compound used in making soap, fertilizer, fiberglass, and other products. Borax mining in Death Valley began in 1881, and continues today.

In the early days, the borax was hauled to a distant railroad in huge wooden wagons.

Prospectors mined fields of
borax instead of the gold and
silver they hoped to find.

Twenty-mule teams (above) hauled tons of borax to the railroad. Equipment that was used during the 1800s borax boom (right).

Each wagon, pulled by a team of 20 mules, carried 20 tons of borax.

Today, at the Borax Museum at Furnace Creek Ranch, you can see the actual equipment used during the 1800s borax boom.

Saved from Destruction

By the early 1900s, mining and other commercial activities threatened to destroy Death Valley's natural beauty. On February 11, 1933, however, President Herbert Hoover made Death Valley a national monument. In 1994, Death Valley was declared a

Death Valley National Park attracts visitors from all over the world.

national park. National parks are protected from commercial development, so that future generations can enjoy these special places. Today, thousands of people come from all around the world to visit Death Valley National Park.

In spite of its name, Death Valley is not always hot and unfriendly. Fall and winter months are pleasant. Spring is especially beautiful when the cacti and wildflowers bloom. They paint the valley with a striking mix of reds, whites, blues, purples, and yellows.

In spring, the barrel cactus blooms with beautiful flowers.

Green Water Valley (left);
Golden Canyon (above)

In fact, Death Valley has as many places named for their beauty as it does for their harshness. Artist's Drive, Green Water Valley, and canyons called Wildrose, Mosaic, and Golden are just a few such spots.

When You Visit

The Furnace Creek Visitor Center is located near the center of Death Valley. There, displays, slide programs, publications, and friendly park rangers will introduce you to this unique national park.

From the Visitor Center, several roadside view points are

At Furnace Creek Visitor Center (above), rangers are available to answer visitors' questions (right).

a short drive away. One of the most popular is Dante's View, which looks down on Badwater.

A favorite among Death Valley's natural wonders is Ubehebe Crater, located at the north end of the park. This

Dante's View (left); Ubehebe Crater (above) is one of the most popular sites in Death Valley National Park.

crater was created about a thousand years ago when steam exploded from deep within the Earth. Ubehebe is 750 feet (229 m) deep and almost half a mile (0.8 km) wide.

A short drive from Ubehebe Crater is the Racetrack, which is really a dry lake bed. There you'll see one of the world's most amazing sights—huge rocks, some weighing hundreds of pounds, which have moved as far as 500 yards (457 m) apparently by themselves! The rocks have left trails in the dried mud of the lake bed as evidence of their movement.

What makes the rocks move? When rain hits the lake bed, the mud becomes very

Rocks seem to move by themselves across the Racetrack.

slick. Then, strong winds of up to 50 miles (80 km) per hour push the rocks along, like stone sailboats on a shallow lake.

Take a Hike

If you enjoy clean, fresh air and exercise, you'll want to hike a few of the park's self-guiding trails.

In nature, the most interesting sights and experiences often wait beyond the roads. This is especially true at Death Valley. In winter, ranger-guided walks are conducted daily.

Hiking (left) and camping (top right) are fun ways to enjoy Death Valley. Furnace Creek Inn (bottom right)

After an active day of exploring, you can pitch your tent at your choice of nine campgrounds. Or you can rent a room at one of the park's two resorts.

Scotty's Castle

Strangely enough, the most famous of Death Valley's attractions is not natural, but manmade. It is called Scotty's Castle.

Walter E. Scott—known as "Death Valley Scotty"—was born in Kentucky in 1872. When he was only eleven years old, he and his brothers went west in search of adventure.

Eventually, Scotty wound up in Death Valley. He claimed to have discovered a gold mine, but most likely, it was only a story he made up. He hoped to get money from wealthy people who thought they were investing in the gold mine.

One of Scotty's investors was a Chicago millionaire named Albert Johnson. Over several years, Johnson gave

Scotty thousands of dollars to develop the mine. Scotty, however, apparently spent the money on himself.

Finally, Johnson visited Death Valley, with Scotty acting as his guide. Johnson never did see the "gold mine" he had invested so much money in, but he fell in love with Death Valley and became good friends with Scotty.

In 1915, Johnson bought land in Grapevine Canyon and built a huge, Spanish-style mansion complete with towers and fourteen fireplaces. He called it Death Valley Ranch.

Always eager to get his name in the news, Scotty boasted that it was his "castle." Newspapers printed the story, and that is how "Scotty's Castle" got its name.

Scotty's Castle

In 1970, Scotty's Castle was purchased by the United States government and became part of Death Valley National Monument. Visitors can tour this historic building any day of the year.

A Protected Environment

In 1985, the United Nations included Death Valley in the Mojave Biosphere Preserve. This protection helps ensure that Death Valley National Park will always be as beautiful—and as wild—as it is today. And because it is a preserved area, you and your family will be able to visit and enjoy Death Valley for years to come.

The Mojave

Death Valley National Park

The land, plants and animals in a biosphere preserve are protected from harm. As a result, scientists can study their natural surroundings. The Mojave Biosphere Preserve, which includes Death Valley National Park, is a fascinating world of salt flats, lava flows, limestone caves, and old mines.

Biosphere Preserve

It is home to Joshua trees, desert tortoises, and black-tailed jackrabbits. Within the preserve, you can visit the "singing" sand dunes at Kelso, the crumbling ruins of Fort Paiute, and a town called Zzyzx.

To Find Out More

Here are some additional resources to help you learn more about Death Valley National Park.

 **Books**

 **Organizations**

Brown, Richard, illus. **A Kid's Guide to National Parks.** 1989. Harcourt Brace.

Fradin, Dennis. **California.** 1992. Children's Press.

Lovett, Sarah. **Kidding Around the National Parks of the Southwest: A Young Person's Guide.** 1990. John Muir.

Salts, Bobbi. **Death Valley Discovery!** 1991. Death Valley Natural History Association.

Weber, Michael. **Our National Parks.** 1994. Millbrook Press.

Death Valley National Park
Death Valley, CA 92328
619-786-2331

National Park Service
Office of Public Inquiries
P.O. Box 37127
Washington, DC 20013
202-208-4747

Western Region
National Park Service
600 Harrison Street
Suite 600
San Francisco, CA 94107

National Parks and Conservation Association
1776 Massachusetts
  Avenue, NW
Washington, DC 20036
800-NAT-PARK
natparks@aol.com
npca@npca.org

Online Sites

Great Outdoor Recreation Pages (GORP)
http://www.gorp.com/gorp/resource/US_National_Park/main.htm

Information on hiking, fishing, boating, climate, places to stay, plant life, wildlife, and more.

National Park Foundation
CompuServe offers online maps, park products, special programs, a question-and-answer series, and in-depth information available by park name, state, region, or interest. From the main menu, select *Travel*, then *Where to Go*, then *Complete Guide to America's National Parks.*

National Park Service World Wide Web Server
http://www.nps.gov

Includes virtual tours, maps, essays.

National Parks Magazine
editorial@npca.org

Focuses on the park system in general, as well as on individual sites.

Note: Many of the national parks have their own home pages on the World Wide Web. Do some exploring!

Important Words

crater bowl-shaped hole made by the eruption of a volcano

hemisphere one-half of the Earth; the western hemisphere includes North and South America

mammals animals that give birth to live young and nurse their offspring

predators animals that kill and eat other animals to survive

prospector person in search of gold, silver, or other precious minerals

species kind of plant or animal

ton 2,000 pounds

United Nations group of nations that works for international peace and well-being

Index

Meet the Author

David Petersen lives in the San Juan Mountains of southwestern Colorado. For nearly 20 years, he has explored the western United States and written—for both children and adults—about many of its most interesting places and creatures. He has also written True Books about Bryce Canyon National Park, Denali National Park and Preserve, and Petrified Forest National Park—all available from Children's Press.